Opening up
Malachi

ROGER ELLSWORTH

DayOne

Opening up
Malachi

ROGER ELLSWORTH

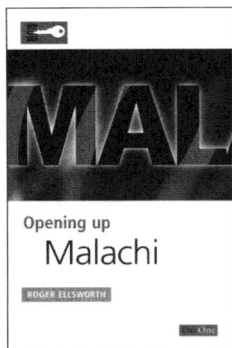

'Arguments and acrimony—the book of Malachi is shot through with them! The Jews, returning from exile, were only too ready to express their grievances against God and to debate with his prophet. Through his spokesman—Malachi—God took these contentions head on and challenged his people to replace a superficial faith for a real and meaningful relationship with him. Roger Ellsworth's insightful exposition of this powerful book shows us that the prophet Malachi has an urgent message to Christians living in the beginning of the twenty-first century.'

Simon J Robinson
Senior Pastor, Walton Evangelical Church, Chesterfield, England

'If you're a busy pastor or a layman who craves theological precision and practical application from a commentary, avail yourself of this book. You will quickly discover that Ellsworth's down-home, easy-to-read presentation of difficult biblical narratives and concepts makes the truth come alive with greater clarity and forcefulness. The scope of this work on Malachi's prophecy is much broader than the book of Malachi itself. It gives the reader a broader understanding of the whole period of the pre-exilic, exilic and post-exilic prophetic ministry, as well as specific interpretive elements of this last revelation of the Old Testament period. I thoroughly recommend this book as a splendid addition to the library of anyone serious about the study of God's Word.'

Dr Roy Hargrave
Senior Pastor, Riverbend Community Church, Ormond Beach, Florida

© Day One Publications 2007
First printed 2007

ISBN 978-1-84625-033-0

9 781846 250330 >

British Library Cataloguing in Publication Data available

Published by Day One Publications
Ryelands Road, Leominster, HR6 8NZ
Telephone 01568 613 740   FAX 01568 611 473

email—sales@dayone.co.uk
web site—www.dayone.co.uk
North American—e-mail-sales@dayonebookstore.com
North American web site—www.dayonebookstore.com

Designed by Steve Devane and printed by Gutenberg Press, Malta

*The following pages are dedicated to
Larry and Kaye Miller
who are part of both my families—earthly and heavenly.*

*I also appreciate the members of my Sanctuary Bible Class
who have allowed me to share with them the lectures from
which the following chapters sprang.
The interest of these people in Bible teaching is a constant
source of blessing to me.*

*As always, I am much indebted to my wife, Sylvia, who
encourages and helps me in more ways than I can enumerate.*

List of Bible abbreviations

THE OLD TESTAMENT		1 Chr.	1 Chronicles	Dan.	Daniel
		2 Chr.	2 Chronicles	Hosea	Hosea
Gen.	Genesis	Ezra	Ezra	Joel	Joel
Exod.	Exodus	Neh.	Nehemiah	Amos	Amos
Lev.	Leviticus	Esth.	Esther	Obad.	Obadiah
Num.	Numbers	Job	Job	Jonah	Jonah
Deut.	Deuteronomy	Ps.	Psalms	Micah	Micah
Josh.	Joshua	Prov.	Proverbs	Nahum	Nahum
Judg.	Judges	Eccles.	Ecclesiastes	Hab.	Habakkuk
Ruth	Ruth	S.of.S.	Song of Solomon	Zeph.	Zephaniah
1 Sam.	1 Samuel	Isa.	Isaiah	Hag.	Haggai
2 Sam.	2 Samuel	Jer.	Jeremiah	Zech.	Zechariah
1 Kings	1 Kings	Lam.	Lamentations	Mal.	Malachi
2 Kings	2 Kings	Ezek.	Ezekiel		

THE NEW TESTAMENT		Gal.	Galatians	Heb.	Hebrews
		Eph.	Ephesians	James	James
Matt.	Matthew	Phil.	Philippians	1 Peter	1 Peter
Mark	Mark	Col.	Colossians	2 Peter	2 Peter
Luke	Luke	1 Thes.	1 Thessalonians	1 John	1 John
John	John	2 Thes.	2 Thessalonians	2 John	2 John
Acts	Acts	1 Tim.	1 Timothy	3 John	3 John
Rom.	Romans	2 Tim.	2 Timothy	Jude	Jude
1 Cor.	1 Corinthians	Titus	Titus	Rev.	Revelation
2 Cor.	2 Corinthians	Philem.	Philemon		

Overview

The little prophecy of Malachi occupies a unique position. It is the last book of the Old Testament era, and it is the beginning of a four-hundred-year period in which God gave no fresh revelation. When God spoke again, it was to announce that he was only mere months away from keeping the promise that he had made very early in human history. That promise was to send his Son, the Messiah.

The coming of the Lord Jesus was simultaneously a vindication and an indictment. The vindication belonged to God. The time between the giving of the promise and the fulfilment of it was so long that it often appeared that it was all a pipe dream. The coming of Christ triumphantly proclaimed the complete and utter faithfulness of God. The indictment belongs to all those who doubted God's promise.

Malachi's prophecy is not a dead message to people of a long ago time. It still lives! Written so very long ago, it addresses the people of God today with a power that shows that it came from God. The prophet ministered at a time when vibrant faith was rare, and crippling doubt was common. It was an era in which people were more often than not weary in spiritual things, eager to embrace the easy way out, and careless and casual about the commandments of the Lord.

MEDITERRANEAN SEA

BETHEL

JERICHO

JERUSALEM

BETHLEHEM

HEBRON

SALT SEA

BEERSHEBA

EDOM

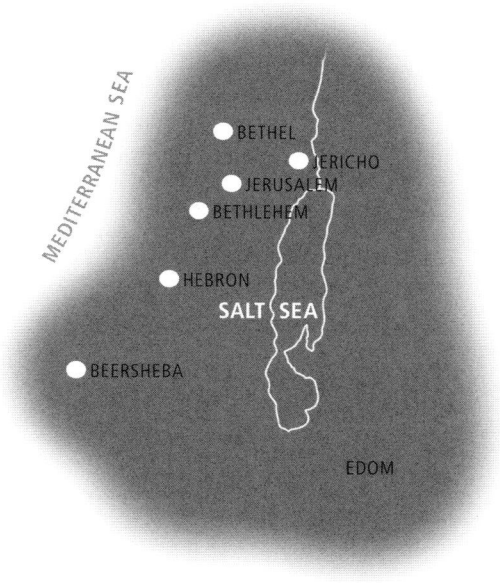

CYRUS ISSUES THE DECREE PERMITTING
THE JEWS TO RETURN TO THEIR HOMELAND

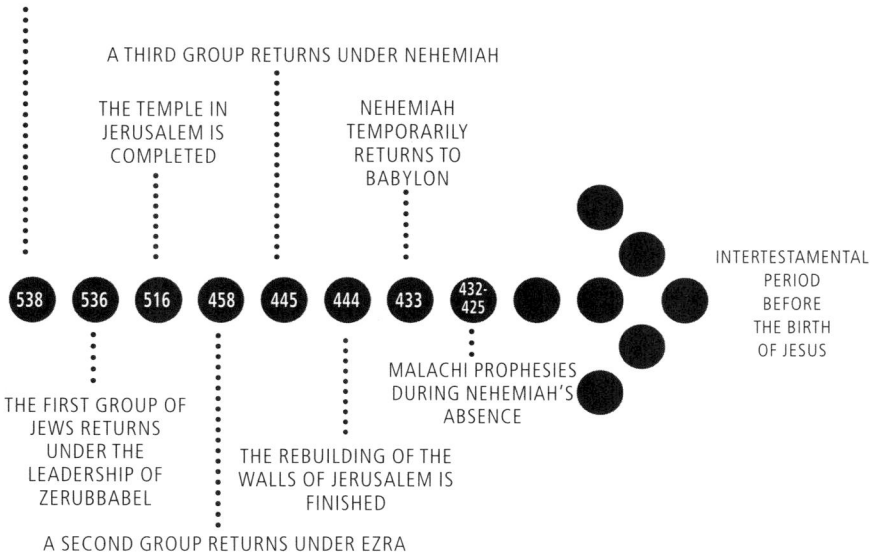

A THIRD GROUP RETURNS UNDER NEHEMIAH

THE TEMPLE IN
JERUSALEM IS
COMPLETED

NEHEMIAH
TEMPORARILY
RETURNS TO
BABYLON

538 536 516 458 445 444 433 432-425

INTERTESTAMENTAL
PERIOD
BEFORE
THE BIRTH
OF JESUS

THE FIRST GROUP OF
JEWS RETURNS
UNDER THE
LEADERSHIP OF
ZERUBBABEL

MALACHI PROPHESIES
DURING NEHEMIAH'S
ABSENCE

THE REBUILDING OF THE
WALLS OF JERUSALEM IS
FINISHED

A SECOND GROUP RETURNS UNDER EZRA

The parallels between that time and our own are easy enough to see if we care to look. As the people of that generation were called to live on the basis of the Word of God without miraculous confirmations of the truth of that Word, so are we. As they awaited the promise of the Messiah's first coming, so we await the promise of his second coming. And as their faith often flickered and their performance often faltered, so do ours.

But we don't have to be like the people of Malachi's time. He called his people to faith in the God who had so often proved himself faithful to them and who would do so again. We can heed that call and live in the faith for which he called.

Background and summary

When we hear the name 'Malachi', many of us think of the last book of the Old Testament. Useful information for winning a point in a Bible trivia game! Few realize that Malachi conveys a message that is of critical importance.

The time of Malachi's ministry

The prophets of the Old Testament fall into three categories. Pre-exilic prophets are those who prophesied before the exile, or captivity (e.g., Isaiah, Micah, Jeremiah). Exilic prophets are those who prophesied during the captivity (e.g., Daniel, Ezekiel). Post-exilic prophets are those who prophesied after the people returned to their homeland. Malachi is one of the post-exilic prophets.

The captivity refers, of course, to the period the Jewish people spent in Babylon. This captivity came about in three stages or installments.

IN 605 B.C., some Jews were taken into captivity, including Daniel and his friends, Shadrach, Meshach and Abed-Nego.

IN 597 B.C., ten thousand more Jews were taken, including Jehoiachin the king of Judah and Ezekiel the prophet (2 Kings 24:1-16).

IN 586 B.C., the Babylonian army, under King Nebuchadnezzar, destroyed the city of Jerusalem and took captive practically all of the remaining citizens, including

King Zedekiah (2 Kings 25).

The Babylonian Captivity came to an end when Babylon was conquered by Persia, and Cyrus the king issued a decree that released the Jews (538 B.C.).

But just as the Jews went into captivity at different times, so they returned. The first return, consisting of 50,000, was led by Zerubbabel, the grandson of King Jehoiachin, in 536 B.C. (Ezra 1:5-2:70; Neh. 12).

Two of the major accomplishments of this group of returnees were rebuilding the temple and restoring the sacrificial system (516 B.C.).

In 458 B.C., Ezra the priest led a second group. In 445 B.C., Nehemiah led yet another group. Nehemiah was appointed governor of the Jewish nation by King Artaxerxes of Persia.

Things progressed rapidly under Nehemiah. The walls of Jerusalem were rebuilt, and a spiritual renewal took place.

But Nehemiah was called back to Persia on business and was absent from Jerusalem from 432-425 B.C. (Neh. 2:6; 5:14; 13:6). Malachi conducted his ministry during those years.

The mood of Malachi's time

As noted above, the temple had been rebuilt and the sacrifices had resumed before Malachi came on the scene. The walls of Jerusalem had also been constructed. Many good things had been achieved in the long, tortuous task of rebuilding the nation.

But while good things had happened, Malachi's was not a good time. Miles Bennett describes the situation in this way:

A spirit of dull depression had settled over the inhabitants of Jerusalem; skepticism and spiritual indifference held the people in their grasp. ... The flood of skepticism abroad in the land affected both the people and their religious leaders. Religion became largely a matter of ritual. Apathy and stinginess toward God prevailed.[1]

How did the people get into such a state? Two prophets, Haggai and Zechariah, had promised that the temple would indeed surpass Solomon's (Hag. 2:1-9). The people concluded that the only way for this to happen would be for the Messiah himself to come and make the temple glorious by his presence. Years passed and the people had not seen anything that looked like a fulfilment of the prophecies of Zechariah and Haggai.

Joyce Baldwin writes: ' ... the Temple had been completed, but nothing momentous had occurred to indicate that God's presence had returned to fill it with glory.'[2]

Consequently, in the words of Baldwin, 'The round of religious duties continued to be carried on, but without enthusiasm.'[3]

These people were called upon to live upon the bare word of God until he would again move

> These people were called upon to live upon the bare word of God until he would again move mightily in their midst, but they were finding this to be very difficult. They longed for manifestations of God's power and, when these were not forthcoming, they became weary of performing their duties.

mightily in their midst, but they were finding this to be very difficult. They longed for manifestations of God's power and, when these were not forthcoming, they became weary of performing their duties.

The Book of Malachi is shocking. We are surprised to find the Jewish nation in such a terrible state after the Babylonian Captivity. By the time Malachi came on the scene, the captivity had been over for more than one hundred years. Although that is a substantial period of time, the captivity was such a traumatic event that we should think its lessons would not have been forgotten. But the people of Malachi's generation were showing signs of doing that very thing. The nation began to disregard her special covenant relationship with God (1:1-5) as both priests (1:6-2:9) and people plunged into sinful behaviour (2:10-3:15).

> While they kept up the various religious observances the priests and people quite obviously did not have their hearts in what they were doing.

While they kept up the various religious observances the priests and people quite obviously did not have their hearts in what they were doing. The priests brought defiled sacrifices to God and complained about how tiresome the religious duties were (1:7-8,13). Meanwhile the people thought nothing at all about disregarding God's laws regarding marriage (2:14-16) or about withholding their tithes (3:8-10). They also regarded service to God as vain and meaningless (3:13-15). Furthermore, the people seem to have all but lost faith in the coming of their Messiah (3:1).

The message for the mood

God's answer to the condition of the people was to send Malachi to carry on a dialogue with the people. There are seven occurrences of dialogue in which God makes an accusation, the people raise an objection and God refutes the objection (1:2-5; 1:6-8; 1:12-14; 2:10-16; 2:17-3:6; 3:7-12; 3:13-15).

It is interesting to observe that the Lord addresses his people in the first person. This suggests, in the words of Joyce Baldwin, 'a vivid encounter between God and the people, unsurpassed in the prophetic books.'4

Using the dialogue method, Malachi confronts the priests and the people with their sins. He affirms that the promised Messiah was indeed coming, but he warns that this coming would not be a happy event for sinful people (3:1-6; 4:1-6).

Is Malachi a message for us?

All that we have established may seem to suggest that Malachi is an appropriate topic of study only for those who have a quaint interest in ancient history. A prophet preaching to people who lived 2400 years ago surely has no value or meaning for us!

But it does! Yes, Malachi's message is dated, but it is not out of date. While times have changed, many things have not. God's people today know the very same God as Malachi and the people of faith in his day. We have been redeemed by the same grace as they, and we struggle with the same problems. We must say, therefore, that we can ignore Malachi only if we never waver in our faith, never offer half-hearted devotion to the Lord and never ignore his commandments.

Malachi will find us out and help us out. He will show us what is going wrong in our hearts and tell us how to fix it. He will tell us if we are sick and prescribe good medicine for us. Let's walk with him for a while.

FOR FURTHER STUDY

1. Read 2 Kings 24:1-16. What does this passage tell us about the Babylonian Captivity?
2. Read Jeremiah 23:28. What is the prophet's role?

TO THINK ABOUT AND DISCUSS

1. Why do you think it is important to study the prophecy of Malachi? Suggest at least five reasons that show its relevance to modern life.
2. Malachi's time was one of apathy. What signs of apathy do you see in the church today?

1 Doubting God's love

(1:1-5)

God has spoken (v. 1)

The word of the Lord comes to Israel through his prophet, Malachi. So the prophet, speaking under the inspiration of the Holy Spirit, begins his prophecy by identifying three matters of vital importance:

The reason for the prophecy

Malachi spoke because he could not help but speak. 'The burden of the word of the LORD' was upon him.

Malachi did not begin his message by saying, 'I have been thinking about some things and would like to share them with you.' He did not say: 'It seems to me...'

His message was laid upon him by the Lord, and it was pressing upon him. It lay upon him like a weight, and the only way he could get any relief from the pressure was to declare it faithfully.

God still has a message of truth for people today. It is a message about human sin that calls for divine judgement. It is a message about forgiveness of sins through the redeeming work of Jesus. It is a message of enormous importance, but few seem to feel the weight of it. Sadly enough, even preachers often do not give the appearance of feeling the weight of truth. They breezily enter their pulpits to smile agreeably at their people and give them a few tips on this or that, making sure as they do so, that they generously sprinkle in words that are bound to get some chuckles. Who would guess that they have been charged to stand before an eternity-bound people on behalf of the eternal God with the express purpose of preparing the former to meet the latter!

Malachi had read the Word of God and had read the people of God. And the gap between the two was great. It was so great that he could not stand idly by. He had to seek to narrow the gap by declaring the Word to the people. A pressured man pressuring a casual people to feel the weight of the truth—that is Malachi!

The recipients of the prophecy

Malachi's message is addressed to 'Israel'. After the death of Solomon, that name applied only to the ten tribes that made up the Northern Kingdom, with the two tribes of the Southern Kingdom being called 'Judah'. But after the captivity ended, the nation, no longer divided, was Israel once again.

The deliverer of the prophecy

The word of the Lord was coming to Israel through Malachi. The name means 'My messenger'. Some have expressed the opinion that there was no prophet with this name, and that it may have been a nickname for Ezra. But in the absence of any evidence to the contrary, we should assume that there was actually a prophet named 'Malachi', who was indeed God's messenger to the nation.

Having tightly packaged this basic information into a few words, Malachi plunges into his message. We have noted that dialogue is the vehicle he uses to convey God's message to the people of Israel, and we have noted that each dialogue consists of the Lord making an assertion, the people objecting to that assertion and the Lord defending it.

Malachi wasted no time in employing this device. After stating that the 'burden' of the word of God was resting on him (v. 1), he stated the Lord's assertion: 'I have loved you' (v. 2).

And, astonishingly, the people responded: 'In what way have you loved us?' (v. 2).

The love of God for his people is so great that it would seem to be beyond question, but these people did question it. And many are questioning it today. They look beyond a thousand blessings to see one difficulty, and on the basis of that they doubt the love of God.

Refusing to let the doubt of Israel go unanswered, the Lord points to three phases of his love for them.

Love in the past (vv. 2-3)

The fact that they were God's people was proof enough of his love! For them to be his people, they had to be chosen from among others and those others had to be rejected.

The Lord reminds them of this by calling them to think about their father Jacob and his brother Esau.

How is it that Israel was in a special covenant relationship with God? It was because the Lord had made a choice. He chose Jacob and rejected Esau! The Lord's statement that he 'hated' Esau has caused no small amount of consternation among Bible students. What does it mean? Joyce Baldwin offers this explanation:

> The very fact that Jacob was chosen, 'loved', meant that Esau was rejected, 'hated', rejection being implicit in the exercise of choice. Personal animosity towards Esau is not implied. Esau and his descendants, however, by nursing resentment and showing hostility towards Jacob, did bring God's judgement on themselves.[1]

God's love for Israel in the past had also been borne out by his providential care of her. While he had blessed her with the land of Canaan—'flowing with milk and honey'—the descendants of Esau (Edom) had been left without such a land.

Centuries have come and gone since the Lord spoke to Israel through Malachi, but God still says to his people, 'I have loved you.'

One of the most crippling foes we face is familiarity with the truth. Mere mortals can never hear more awesome and astounding words from God than these: 'I have loved you.' To appreciate them we have to think long and hard about the 'I' and the 'you'. The 'I' is none other than the sovereign, holy God who is clothed in majesty and splendour. And the 'you' refers to people, like ourselves, who are sinful, undeserving and worthy only of condemnation. Now listen to it again and marvel: 'I have loved you!' God has loved sinners! Can it be?

How has God demonstrated his love? He has done so by setting his heart on all believers before the world began. He chose them to be his own (Eph. 1:4-6).

But we cannot peer into the misty councils of eternity to see the electing love of God. So where do we look? To the cross of Jesus Christ! As we look there, we must each exclaim: God loved me so much that he nailed his Son to that cross to bear the penalty for my sins!

Jesus affirmed that he loves his people even as the Father had loved him (John 15:9). How has the Father loved the Son? Without measure, without change and without end! The cross shows us that Jesus indeed loves us in the same way.

Sometimes our circumstances are such that we find ourselves wondering if God truly loves us, and the devil is ever eager to tell us that he does not. Our circumstances prove it! But the wise believer points the devil to the cross and says, 'There is where God proved his love for me, and my circumstances, whatever they mean, can never mean that God does not love me.'

Love in the present (v. 4)

Both the descendants of Jacob (Israel) and Esau (Edom) had experienced tough times. Israel had spent seventy years in captivity in Babylon, and Edom had been invaded by the Nabateans and forced from their land to take refuge south of Judah.

But while God, in his love for Israel, was in the process of enabling Israel to rebuild her nation, he was doing no such thing for Edom. God's judgement was continuing to rest on

Edom because of her refusal to see his grace at work in the life of Israel and to submit to it. That refusal revealed Edom to be a very wicked nation and caused the Lord to have indignation against her.

While God's love is most definitely a thing in the past, it is not only in the past. Every child of God drinks from the fountain of his love every day. The truths of his Word, the joys of fellowship with his people, the beauties of his worship, and the assurance of his presence are just a few of the expressions of his ongoing love. To these we can add: his continuing willingness to forgive, his guidance, his readiness to hear our prayers, his sustaining care. These things, richly enjoyed by the people of God, are not experienced by those who do not share their faith.

Love in the future (v. 5)

This verse holds before Israel the coming of a better day ('Your eyes shall see, And you shall say… ').

When would this better day come? Some think it refers to the time of the Maccabean dynasty when the Jews would successfully resist the power of the Grecian Empire and regain some of their former glory.

But the ultimate fulfilment of this promise must be found in the Lord Jesus Christ. Through his redeeming work, he has caused God to be 'magnified beyond the border of Israel'.

The very fact that millions attend church each week to honour Christ constitutes proof that this promise has been and is being fulfilled.

But the promise is going to reach its final fulfilment when the heavenly host and the redeemed of all ages gather round

the throne of God in praise for Christ's redemption (Rev. 5).
That will be as far beyond the borders of Israel as one can get!
That will also be a day when the people of God 'shall see' and
'shall say.' A day of seeing and saying! What will they see?
There will be so much to see in eternal glory, but the most
impressive of all is the seeing of the face of Christ (Rev. 22:4).
And the seeing of our Redeemer will surely cause the
redeemed to say:

> Worthy is the Lamb who was
>   slain
> To receive power and riches
>   and wisdom,
> And strength, and honour and
>   glory and blessing!
> (Rev. 5:12).

The past, present and future expressions of God's love for
his people compel us to join Moses in exclaiming:

> Happy are you, O Israel!
> Who is like you,
> a people saved by the LORD…
> (Deut. 33:29).

FOR FURTHER STUDY

1. Read Romans 9:11-16. What does the apostle Paul identify as the basis of God's love?

2. Read Romans 8:31-39. What does this passage teach about the love of God?

TO THINK ABOUT AND DISCUSS

1. What do you consider to be some indications that a pastor is under 'the burden of the word of the LORD'?

2. What is your response to the evidences of God's love in your life?

2 Dishonouring God's name

(1:6-8)

The faith of the people of Israel during Malachi's day was burning low. God sent the prophet to show the people their condition and to call them back to a vibrant and living faith.

One evidence of their flickering faith was their doubting God's love for them.

The verses above bring us to yet another evidence, namely, their dishonouring of the name of God. This would be astonishing enough if the Lord had raised this issue with the people in general, but he primarily addresses the religious leadership of the nation (1:6; 2:1). Religious leaders with no regard for the name of God! Imagine it!

Why were they to honour God's name? (v. 6)

On the ground of affection

Out of love for their children, fathers provide for their needs and protect them from dangers. The Lord here identifies himself as Israel's father. He has already declared his love for his people (v. 2), and he has given evidences or proofs of that love (vv. 2-5).

What was the proper response to such love? The Lord himself answers, 'A son honours his father... ' (v. 6).

This is generally true. Sons have real affection for their fathers and seek to do things that will honour them. There are, of course, fathers who make themselves unworthy of the respect and affection of their sons, but this was not the case with God. There could never be a better father.

Shockingly enough, the priests responded to the fatherhood of God, not by seeking to honour him, but rather by doing things to dishonour him. The Lord asks, 'Where is my honour?'

On the ground of obligation

The Lord changes the figure by also pointing out that the servant honours his master.

The people of Israel were called to serve the Lord as their Master, and were more obligated to do so than any servant. But they were refusing to show reverence to God. John Benton says, 'Reverence is not the homage which weak minds pay to religious tradition and the status quo; it is rather the loving, sincere and practical recognition of the greatness of God.'[1]

After hearing God's accusation, we might expect the priests to say something along these lines: 'We have been dishonouring God's name? Oh, God, forgive us and help us!'

They responded in a far different way: 'In what way have we despised your name?' (v. 6).

They refused to take the charge home to their hearts, and chose rather to debate with God about it.

These figures have as much meaning and application today

as they did in Malachi's day. The people of God in every generation are in the same relationship to God. We are his children and his servants. We are to love him and to obey him. As we read the Lord's message to Israel of old, we must ask ourselves if we are doing better than they in loving and serving God.

Is the Lord saying to us, 'Where is my honour?' Is he asking, 'Where is my reverence?'

What does the Lord say about our love for him? Is he repeating the words he spoke to the church of Ephesus: ' ... I have this against you, that you have left your first love'? (Rev. 2:4).

Is the Lord asking us the same question that he put before his disciples long ago: 'But why do you call Me "Lord, Lord," and do not do the things which I say?' (Luke 6:46).

How were they dishonouring God's name? (vv. 7-8)

What was God's basis for accusing them of dishonouring his name? Verse 7 tells us that the priests were offering 'defiled food' to God. Verse 8 tells us that they were bringing the blind, the lame and the sick to God.

> They were offering as sacrifices the very animals that were likely to die very soon. Thus they were not really sacrificing anything at all!

They were supposed to bring their best to God, and they were bringing their worst. They were offering as sacrifices the very animals that were likely to die very soon. Thus they were not really sacrificing anything at all! They were essentially saying that God was not worthy of their best.

To drive his point home, the Lord tells them to try the same thing with their governor (v. 8)! No political leader of that day would have been pleased with his people paying their taxes with diseased animals. They would not even try to get by with such a thing! But they were doing it with their supreme ruler!

In telling them to take their worthless offerings to the governor, the Lord gives his people of every era a valuable test by which they can determine how they are going about their service to him: are we trying to pass off on God things we would not dare pass off on a human superior?

Here are some things people often say to excuse themselves from worshipping and serving God:

'I'm tired.'
'I had to do this so much as a child, I got burned out on it.'
'I felt unappreciated.'
'No one spoke to me.'

Would we dare use such excuses with our employers? If not, we should not dare use them with God! John Benton pointedly asks: 'How can we possibly have less respect for the King of kings than we do for the political powers who are appointed by him?'[2]

Are we giving our best to God in worship? Do we arrive on time with hearts that are prepared and eager to worship? Do we concentrate on what we are doing in public worship? Or do we allow our thoughts to wander? Do we give the preaching of God's Word a grateful and careful hearing? Or have we allowed our familiarity with the things of God to dull our appreciation for them? Have we lost the wonder of it all? Have we brought ourselves under the following indictment of the Lord Jesus:

> Hypocrites! Well did Isaiah prophesy about you, saying:
> 'These people draw near to
> Me with their mouth,
> And honour me with their lips,
> But their heart is far from me... '
> (Matt. 15:7-8).

We like to avoid thinking about such things, but the more we avoid them, the more our faith weakens. And the more it weakens, the more we rob ourselves of peace, joy and comfort in the Lord. The way back from a sputtering faith is to stop making excuses for ourselves and recognize again the privilege of having God as our Father and our Master.

1. Read Matthew 22:34-40. What do we learn from these verses about our duty to love God? Read Romans 12:11. How are we to go about serving the Lord?

2. Read Exodus 20:7; Psalm 34:3; 54:6; Matthew 6:9. What responsibilities do we have pertaining to the name of God?

TO THINK ABOUT AND DISCUSS

1. Why should the name of God be precious to us? Identify some ways in which God's name is being dishonoured today.

2. What are some ways in which we can show reverence for the name of God?

3 More about dishonouring God's name

(1:9-11)

In these verses, the Lord continues to rebuke the priests of Israel for their disregard of his name. He does so in two ways. Firstly, he points out the terrible results of their irreverence. Secondly, he proclaims his own commitment to honour his name.

God announces some results of their irreverence (vv. 9-10)

All sin is rooted in disregard or irreverence for God. Those who start down the path of sin often seem to be getting away with it, but no one ever finally gets away with sin. It always carries a price tag! That price must be paid! Sometimes, the price is paid in this life. Sometimes it is paid in eternity. In most cases, it is paid in both. But it is always paid!

The Lord here informs the priests of the price they were paying for their sin.

Unanswered prayer (v. 9)

Their disdain for the name of God resulted in God refusing to answer their prayers!

Malachi seems to dare the priests to check this out for themselves. He essentially says, 'Ask God for something. See if he will be gracious.'

He then solemnly assures them that they cannot ask for God's favour with their mouths while their hands are engaged in dishonouring him.

We do not like to be told that the success of our prayers is tied to the conduct of our lives, but it is a link that the Bible will not let us ignore (Ps. 66:18; Prov. 15:29; 28:9; Isa. 59:1-3).

Our first response to unanswered prayer, therefore, must not be to accuse God of failing to keep his word but rather to examine our hearts to see if we are living according to that word.

This doesn't mean we have to be perfect in order to get our prayers answered. We must clear the channel between God and ourselves if we expect his blessings to flow through. John Benton observes:

> God's answering our prayers does not depend on our being sinless. If this were the case no one would have their prayers answered, for none of us is perfect this side of heaven. However, God's hearing our prayers does depend on our being serious about the fight against sin in our lives. It is not the presence of sin but the *toleration* of sin which shuts down communication with heaven[1] (italics are his).

If we expect God to answer our prayers, we must always include repentance for those things that dishonour and displease him.

The loss of value (v. 10)

This verse adds yet another catastrophic result of the priests' irreverence. Here the Lord tells them that their worship is worthless in his eyes. He even calls for them to shut the doors of the temple! No worship is better than irreverent worship!

We cannot read the Lord's words here without thinking of the similar message delivered by the Lord Jesus to the church of Laodicea: 'I know your works, that you are neither cold nor hot. I could wish you were cold or hot. So then, because you are lukewarm, and neither cold nor hot, I will spew you out of my mouth' (Rev. 3:15-16).

This must not be used as an excuse not to worship. God commands both that we worship him and that we worship him in the right way. And the right way is, of course, that which the Lord Jesus indicated in his conversation with the Samaritan woman: 'God is Spirit, and those who worship him must worship in spirit and truth' (John 4:24).

To worship God in spirit is to worship him with our spirits engaged. It is to worship with our hearts going out after God.

To worship him in truth is to do so according to what he himself has revealed. It is to worship according to the truth of his Word. We are not to include anything in worship that is not clearly sanctioned or warranted by the Word of God, no matter how it attracts crowds and pleases people! The money changers whom Jesus drove from the temple could undoubtedly have argued that their innovation was popular. But it did not please him because it did not correspond to God's revealed truth (John 2:13-17).

Worship from the heart and according to the book (the Bible)—that is the kind of worship that pleases God. We are not left to define worship for ourselves. The Lord Jesus has defined it for us.

God proclaims his commitment to his own name (v. 11)

Twice in this verse the Lord says: 'My name shall be great... .'

The Lord is absolutely committed to bringing glory to his name! Some find this disturbing. If it is wrong for us to seek our glory, why is it not wrong for God to do the same?

The answer is that it is wrong for us to seek our glory because we are sinners. But God, as a perfect being, must seek his own glory. If God did not seek his glory, he would no longer be perfect!

We are face to face here with an awesome truth. God has made us for his glory, and it is our tremendous privilege to live for his glory. But if we refuse to do so, God will still have his glory!

The religious leaders of Malachi's day were refusing to give God glory, but they were not defeating him. They were only hurting themselves. God did not need Israel to give him glory. If Israel would not give him his due, he would receive it from the Gentiles. And he would receive it from them on such a wide scale that it was possible for him to say that he would be receiving glory all the time ('from the rising of the sun, even to its going down') and in 'every place'.

Nothing brings God more glory than the gospel. The gospel is the good news of what he, God, has done in and through his Son, Jesus Christ, to provide forgiveness of sins and eternal life for all who believe in Jesus. The heart of the gospel is Jesus' death on the cross. There he received the wrath of God in the stead of sinners. Because he received it, those sinners never have to receive it. They are freed from the penalty of sin because Jesus endured it on their behalf.

> The cross of Christ glorifies the justice of God in that the penalty God had pronounced upon sin was carried out. It glorifies the grace of God in that it provides the way for sinners to be freed from the penalty of sin. And it glorifies the wisdom of God in that the cross satisfied at one and the same time the seemingly conflicting demands of God's justice and grace.

The cross of Christ glorifies the justice of God in that the penalty God had pronounced upon sin was carried out. It glorifies the grace of God in that it provides the way for sinners to be freed from the penalty of sin. And it glorifies the wisdom of God in that the cross satisfied at one and the same time the seemingly conflicting demands of God's justice and grace.

And God will finally have his glory from each one of us. If we receive and serve him, we will bring glory to his grace. If we refuse to receive and serve him, we will experience his judgement and, in so doing, bring glory to his justice. Even those who dismiss the gospel will be at last compelled to acknowledge Christ. Every knee will eventually bow before him and every tongue confess that he is Lord 'to the glory of God the Father' (Phil. 2:11).

FOR FURTHER STUDY

1. Read Mark 11:25-26; James 1:6-7; 4:3; 1 Peter 3:7; 1 John 5:14-15. What are some things that prevent answered prayer?
2. Read Proverbs 1:7; 8:13; 15:16; 16:6; 19:23. What do these verses teach about fearing or reverencing the Lord?

TO THINK ABOUT AND DISCUSS

1. What is your response to the connection between one's conduct and the effectiveness of one's prayers?
2. Identify some thoughts, words and actions that may be hindering your prayer life. What specific steps could you take in order to correct these? How might you help a Christian friend to work on such an area in his or her life?

4 Sinning against the name of the Lord

(1:12 - 2:3)

These verses continue the theme of the priests of Israel dishonouring the name of God. These verses may be divided into two parts: the repetition of God's charges against them and the announcement of God's curse.

The repetition of God's charges (1:12-13)

They were profaning his name (1:12-13)

The word 'profane' comes from a Hebrew word which means 'to wound or stab'.

What a word to use in connection with the glorious, precious name of God! Wounding it! Stabbing it!

How were the priests profaning God's name? In attitude and action. They were essentially declaring that the 'table' ('altar') of the Lord was contemptible, that is, something which possessed no appeal or value.

By bringing stolen, lame and sick animals (v. 13), they were effectively proclaiming that they put no value at all on the altar of the Lord, that they regarded it as having no meaning.

They were expressing weariness with his name (1:13)

The priests were also sinning against the name of the Lord by openly expressing their unhappiness about having to serve. As they went about their duties they were saying, 'Oh, what a weariness!' To them the service of God was an irksome duty instead of a joyous delight.

The Lord also accuses them of sneering at his service. The word 'sneer' comes from a Hebrew word which means to 'blow away'. We might picture it like this: when someone mentioned their work, they would respond with a heavy sigh, a dismissive wave of the hand and rolling of the eyes.

> Such a reaction would say it all. The service of the Lord was to them a very burdensome, unhappy thing!

Such a reaction would say it all. The service of the Lord was to them a very burdensome, unhappy thing!

We must not read these words without examining ourselves. Are we doing the same things as these priests? As we go about public worship, do we give the impression that the things of God are exceedingly precious and glorious? Or do we give the impression that we are engaged in an unpleasant obligation that must be taken out of the way as quickly as possible? Do we go about our service to the Lord in such a way that we make it appear to be a very unattractive thing and in such a way that we make the things of the world to be very wonderful? Do we show respect for the preaching of God's Word? Or do we, by laughing and talking with those around us, show contempt for it?

The announcement of God's curse (1:14 - 2:3)

The reason for this curse

God could not and would not allow the behaviour of the priests to go unpunished. The reason? While the priests were not committed to his name, God was committed to it! (1:14). God identifies himself as 'the LORD of hosts', that is, the God of all the angels, and affirms that he is 'a great King' whose name is to be 'feared among the nations'.

For God to ignore the disdainful treatment of his great name would amount to him dishonouring his own name and denying his own greatness!

The nature of the curse

THE CURSE OF THEIR BLESSINGS (2:2)

This may very well refer to them losing their livelihood. If the priests gave the people the impression that their inferior animals were acceptable for sacrifice, how long would it be before the people stopped bringing those things on which the priests had to subsist, namely, their sacrifices and tithes?

THE CORRUPTING OF THEIR SEED (2:3)

Their flippant attitude towards God and his service would have a detrimental effect on their children. We can rest assured that our children are well aware of whether the things of God are a burden or a blessing to us.

It is a sobering thought to contemplate how many children of pastors have little or no interest in spiritual things because of what they have seen and not seen in the lives of their fathers. Every pastor would do well to consider that he has a congregation at home as well as at church. If the one at home is to turn out well, the children must be able to see that their fathers' hearts are sincere and true, hearts that truly delight in the things of God. If our children detect that we are mere religious professionals who unfeelingly handle spiritual things, it will not go well with them.

THE HUMILIATION AND REJECTION OF THE PRIESTS (2:3)

The Lord says he will 'spread refuse' on the faces of the priests. He would cover them with shame and make them a stench! And just as the refuse of animals has to be carried away, so the Lord would make sure that the priests themselves would be set aside. Miles Bennett writes: 'The defiled priests, unfit for the demands of duty, will be carried off and deposited with dung on the city dumping grounds... Thus they will be utterly disgraced and dishonored.'[1]

> Sinful behaviour can be forgiven if we will listen and change. But if we refuse to listen and press firmly ahead, we invite disaster.

All of these terrible things would come upon them because they would not hear the Lord's words and take them 'to heart' (2:2). Sinful behaviour can be forgiven if we will listen and change. But if we refuse to listen and press firmly ahead, we invite disaster. Old timers used to speak of 'leaning into the Word'. What do our hearts tell us about ourselves? Are we leaning into the Word or away from it?

We surely cannot come away from the colossal failure of the priests of Malachi's day without being thankful for the Lord Jesus Christ. He was the faithful high priest who did nothing but honour the name of God (Heb. 4:14 - 5:5).

FOR FURTHER STUDY

1. Read 1 Corinthians 15:58; Galatians 6:9 and 2 Thessalonians 3:13. What do these verses tell us about serving the Lord?

2. Read Psalm 84. What does this psalm teach about the worship of God?

TO THINK ABOUT AND DISCUSS

1. What are some ways today in which God's people are expressing weariness in their service to the Lord?

2. How can we make sure that we are 'leaning into' the Word instead of leaning away from it? Psalm 1 gives clear teaching on how to be blessed by meditating (reflecting or pondering) on the Word of God. What specific steps could you take to improve your daily reading and practice of Scripture in the light of such a psalm?

5 Corrupting the covenant

(2:4-9)

The Lord had promised to visit judgement on the priests of Israel for their sins. His purpose in doing so was that his covenant with Levi, the tribe of priests, might continue (v. 4). In other words, the judgement would not be a matter of God being mean and spiteful. It would rather be for the beneficial purpose of correcting the priests and bringing them back to what they ought to be.

> One of the most productive lies of the devil is that God enjoys making life miserable for human beings, that he gives us certain rules to spoil our happiness.

The word 'covenant' is the key to the above verses. A covenant is an agreement between two or more people in which each pledges to do or not to do certain things. John Benton writes: 'There is no record in the Old Testament of God making a covenant with Levi in the formal sense. But what Malachi has in mind is the God-given appointment of the tribe of Levi to the priesthood (Jeremiah 33:21).'[1]

We can divide the Lord's words about this covenant into three parts: the purpose of it, the initial performance of it and the present perversion of it.

The purpose of the covenant (v. 5)

To give life and peace

One of the most productive lies of the devil is that God enjoys making life miserable for human beings, that he gives us certain rules to spoil our happiness.

The truth of the matter is, of course, just the opposite. The laws of God are designed, not to destroy our happiness, but rather to secure it. Such was the case with God's covenant with the Levites. By obeying it, they would bring both life and peace to the nation and to themselves. By disobeying it, they would bring destruction and unrest.

To produce fear of God

To fear God is to stand in awe of him. It is to revere his person, to submit to his authority and to dread his displeasure. This may seem to run counter to our happiness, but it is not. The more we stand in awe of God, the more likely we are to obey, and the more we obey the more happiness we find.

The original performance of the covenant (v. 6)

This verse takes us to the past (note the verbs: 'was,' 'walked,' 'turned'). It takes us to that time in which the priesthood was set up under Moses. John Benton notes that those priests, after the horrendous affair of the golden calf (Exod. 32), ' ...

responded to God with reverence and stood in awe of him.'
He further says of those priests:

> They had a holy seriousness and deep respect towards the things of God. Their top priority was not that all the congregation should have a bit of fun. They knew they were engaged in business for eternity. They took great care how they behaved, living all their lives under the eye of the holy God.[2]

In particular, those priests spoke in the right way, having 'the law of truth' on their lips and refusing to speak evil (v. 6). They also behaved in the right way, walking before the Lord 'in peace and equity' (v. 6). They were also used of God to influence others, turning them away from iniquity (v. 6).

The present perversion of the covenant (vv. 7-9)

The prophet cites four ways in which the priests were failing to measure up.

They had 'departed from the way' (v. 8)

This way is described in verse 7. The priests were to 'keep knowledge'. They were to be a reservoir of the knowledge of God and were faithfully to declare that message to others. They were to be God's messengers. They were not free to devise or fashion their own message to suit their own whims or to fit in with the times.

While the priests of Moses' era walked this path, the priests of Malachi's era were straying. The people could not come to them for the Word of God! We might think of the truth of God as rain from heaven. The priests were to be cisterns to receive and store it, but they were more like roofs that shed it! Or, if they were cisterns at all, they were cracked (Jer. 2:13), and could not retain the truth. The Word of God was being lost.

What is the state of things today? Is the current crop of preachers more like those of Moses' era or Malachi's? When people come to church these days, are they hearing sermons that faithfully declare the Word of God?

Steven Lawson offers this assessment of many pastors:

In their zeal to lead popular and successful ministries, many are becoming less concerned with pointing to the biblical text. Their use of the Bible is much like the singing of the national anthem before a ball game—something merely heard at the beginning, but never referenced again, a necessary preliminary that becomes an awkward intrusion into the real event. In their attempt to be contemporary and relevant, many pastors talk about the Scriptures, but, sadly, they rarely speak from them. Instead, they rush headlong to the next personal illustration, humorous anecdote, sociological quote, or cultural reference, rarely to return to the biblical text. How can pastors expect dying souls to become spiritually healthy if they never give them the prescribed remedy? How can pastors expect sinners to be converted and Christians to be sanctified if they fail to expound God's Word ... ?[3]

Lawson then adds these words from Merrill Unger:

To an alarming extent the glory is departing from the pulpit... The basic reason for this gloomy condition is obvious. That which imparts the glory has been taken away from the center of so much of our modern preaching and placed on the periphery. The Word of God has been denied the throne and given a subordinate place.[4]

Here is a man who is struggling. He has walked the paths of sin, but he is dissatisfied. He knows that he must leave this world and meet God, and he knows that he is not prepared for that meeting. The very thought of it frightens him. What can he do? He decides to go to church. The preacher there will surely know how a person can be right with God and will surely be able to declare it! So he goes with hope, but, to his surprise, he finds nothing. The preacher is dabbling in the shallows, functioning as something of a pop psychologist. He gives the impression that he himself is not a man of eternity, but rather just another man of this world. So our struggling man leaves to struggle further. He came to the cistern, but it was dry! The water of truth had seeped out the cracks! The preacher had departed from the way!

They had 'caused many to stumble at the law' (v. 8)

By misinterpreting the laws of God, the priests had caused many to fall into sin. Instead of guiding the people into righteousness, they had 'taught' in such a way as to lead them into error. But there is more here than wrong teaching. They had also lived in such a way as to encourage wrong doing.

Jesus reserved some of his sternest words for those who cause others to stumble:

But whoever causes one of these little ones who believe in me to sin, it would be better for him if a millstone were hung around his neck, and he were drowned in the depth of the sea. Woe to the world because of offences! For offences must come, but woe to that man by whom the offence comes (Matt. 18:6-7).

To the religious leaders of his time, the Lord Jesus spoke these words: 'But woe to you, scribes and Pharisees, hypocrites! For you shut up the kingdom of heaven against men; for you neither go in yourselves, nor do you allow those who are entering to go in' (Matt. 23:13).

They had shown 'partiality in the law' (v. 9)

To endear themselves to some of high standing, the priests had downplayed or modified the demands of God's laws. Pastors today are certainly not beyond this temptation!

They had 'corrupted the covenant of Levi' (vv. 8-9)

By their failures the priests of Israel had spoiled or ruined the very covenant that was intended to bring life and peace. They had

> We cannot leave Malachi's scalding and blistering assessment of the priests without gratefully recalling a priest at the other end of the spectrum. The Lord Jesus Christ performed perfectly in every area in which the priests of Malachi's generation failed.

failed to live up to their part of the agreement. Such failure God could not and would not ignore! His judgement was already at work in this way—the priests had lost standing in the eyes of the people (v. 9). Joyce Baldwin writes: 'The common people recognized godliness when they saw it, and were not slow to scorn the hypocrisy of compromising priests.'5

We cannot leave Malachi's scalding and blistering assessment of the priests without gratefully recalling a priest at the other end of the spectrum. The Lord Jesus Christ performed perfectly in every area in which the priests of Malachi's generation failed. He never departed from the path of obedience to God (1 Peter 1:19; 1 John 3:5). He never misrepresented the truth of God in word or in deed and never misled anyone in spiritual matters. He never compromised the truth in order to curry favour with the rich and the powerful. He in no way corrupted the covenant God had made with those in the priestly office.

Because Jesus perfectly discharged the office of high priest, we can rest assured that the sacrifice he offered for sinners—himself!—has been accepted by God. We can also rest assured that he has been received by the Father in heaven and he is there now to make intercession for all who believe (Heb. 7:25-27) and to sympathize lovingly with his people (Heb. 4:14-16). Furthermore, we can be confident that he will continue to function as our high priest because, by his resurrection, he has proved that he possesses 'the power of an endless life' (Heb. 7:16).

FOR FURTHER STUDY

1. Read 2 Timothy 4:1-5. What is required of pastors?
2. Read Jeremiah 23:9-29. What does this passage teach about false prophets?

TO THINK ABOUT AND DISCUSS

1. Think about the public ministry of Jesus. What characterized it?
2. What is your assessment of the preaching that you are hearing? To what does it give prominence? How could you encourage your minister to be engaged in preaching that consistently honours God and keeps the text of Scripture central in people's minds?

6 Dealing treacherously

(2:10-16)

These verses bring us to a major juncture in the prophecy of Malachi. Here the prophet turns the spotlight from the religious leadership of Israel to the people in general. Given the failure of the priests to lead the nation by offering proper teaching and by modelling correct living, we are not at all surprised that the people in general were far from God.

The lack of leadership did not excuse the people themselves from responsibility. So the Lord now confronts them with their sins, using the same vehicle of dialogue that he has used with the priests.

The dialogue in the passage before us is about loss—terrible loss. It gives us the sad account of the people coming to the altar of the Lord with tears streaming down their cheeks only to have the Lord turn away from them in displeasure (v. 13).

What was going on here? We have a tendency to think that just going to the house of God ought to be enough to please him, but these people were doing more than that. They were actually showing emotion while there. But God was not impressed with either their presence or their emotion.

Through his prophet, the Lord puts his finger on the reason he was rejecting their religious efforts. The Lord accuses them of dealing 'treacherously'. That word appears five times in verses 10-16. It means 'deceitfully'. It is the opposite of acting with integrity or with dependability.

Three major truths emerge from this passage and call for our attention.

The major manifestation of treacherous dealing

We may rest assured that while this treacherous dealing ran through every part of their society, there was a manifestation of it that was particularly unsavoury to the Lord. The prophet calls it an 'abomination' that 'profaned' the Lord's institution (v. 11).

He then proceeds to identify this abomination. He says the nation 'has married the daughter of a foreign god' (v. 11).

A bit later the prophet says the men of the nation have dealt treacherously with the wives of their youth (v. 14).

Evidently the men of Israel were now divorcing their elderly Jewish wives in order to marry younger and more attractive women from surrounding nations. In doing this, they were guilty of both the sin of mixed marriage and the sin of broken marriage.

Mixed marriages (v. 11)

Israel's covenant relationship with God meant he was their God and they were his people. To safeguard that relationship God commanded them not to intermarry with the surrounding nations who worshipped other gods (Deut. 7:3-4).

But this forbidden practice had now become so widespread that the prophet could legitimately say that the whole nation of Judah had 'profaned' the Lord's institution. What was Malachi saying? The Lord's institution was his covenant relationship with his people, whom he loved, and that relationship was now being contaminated by the men of the nation treating their marriages so casually.

The modern equivalent to a mixed marriage is a believer marrying an unbeliever. The apostle Paul pointedly says:

> Do not be unequally yoked together with unbelievers. For what fellowship has righteousness with lawlessness? And what communion has light with darkness? And what accord has Christ with Belial? Or what part has a believer with an unbeliever? And what agreement has the temple of God with idols? For you are the temple of the living God. As God has said:
> 'I will dwell in them
> And walk among them.
> I will be their God,
> And they shall be my people'
> (2 Cor. 6:14-16).

Broken marriages (vv. 14,16)

As we have noted, the men of Israel were divorcing their wives so they could be joined in these mixed marriages. This blatant disregard for their marriage vows, prompted God to say that he hates divorce (v. 16). It violates his ideal of oneness (vv. 10, 15; Gen. 2:24).

To say God hates divorce is to say that he hates everything

that leads up to divorce, which means he also hates all our failures to work towards real companionship and oneness in marriage.

We may be inclined to think that what goes on in our homes doesn't have any bearing on the rest of life, but it does. Here in Malachi's day we find men going to meet the Lord at the temple, and the Lord points them back to their homes. Family life colours and influences every other part of life.

The appalling nature of treacherous dealing

Malachi wanted his people to understand that the sin the Lord was charging them with was no small thing. Satan adopts the opposite strategy. He first entices us by telling us that the course of action he is proposing is not sinful. When conscience protests that it is, he then assures us that even though it is sinful, it really doesn't matter all that much.

Malachi underscored the seriousness of what the men of Judah were doing by stressing three items of monumental importance.

The solidarity of the people of God

Malachi begins his discussion of this matter with some searching and probing questions: 'Have we not all one Father? Has not one God created us? Why do we deal treacherously with one another by profaning the covenant of the fathers?' (v. 10).

The men who were guilty of treacherous dealing with their wives would have undoubtedly been quick to insist that their actions affected no one but themselves. But Malachi would have none of it. The people were not only in covenant with

God but also with one another, and every act of unfaithfulness to God weakens and erodes the people of God as a whole. How often people have looked at the sin of one Christian, and said, 'There you have it! That is what all Christians are like!'

Malachi also stressed the appalling nature of their sin by pointing out:

The sacredness of marriage

Marriage is not simply a social arrangement constructed by men. It is the design of God himself (Gen. 2:21-24).

ONE MAN, ONE WIFE

Malachi makes it clear that God not only designed marriage, but he also designed it in a certain way. He calls attention to the fact that at the beginning God created only one companion for Adam. He could, of course, have created many women. Malachi says God had 'a remnant of the Spirit'.

In other words, God's creative acts in no way diminished his power or ability. He still had plenty of power after he created to create more. After he took Eve from Adam's side, God's power was in no way depleted or expended. He could have made more wives for Adam. In making Eve alone, then, the Lord was making it plain that his design for marriage was for a man to have one wife.

TWO INDIVIDUALS, ONE PERSON

There is, however, another dimension to this matter of oneness. God also intended for the two of them to be one.

There is a physical oneness, but it goes beyond that. Oneness in marriage sometimes reaches such proportions that husbands and wives know what the other is thinking and often complete each other's sentences. True oneness is physical, emotional and spiritual.

Now we are in a position to understand why the next verse refers to divorce as a violent act (v. 16). It rips one person apart and makes two.

Finally, Malachi stressed the seriousness of treacherous dealing in marriage by calling attention to:

The potential for harm

HARM TO THE GUILTY PARTY

Malachi makes it clear that disregard for the laws of God can bring harm to the one who is guilty of it. He knew that the Lord can and does chastise his people for sinful living, and he, Malachi, even desired it. He prays: 'May the LORD cut off from the tents of Jacob the man who does this… ' (v. 12).

This may seem to be a harsh thing, but Malachi preferred to see the Lord punish the men who were dealing treacherously rather than the whole nation.

HARM TO THE CHILDREN

Another harmful effect of this faithless dealing had to do with the children involved. Why did God want his people to be faithful to their marriages? Malachi's answer is this: 'He seeks godly offspring' (v. 15).

God himself is faithful, and he desires for us to be faithful as well. One of the ways we learn faithfulness is by seeing it at work in the home. If God had designed marriage in such a way that a man would not have to be faithful to one woman, the offspring of that marriage would not learn faithfulness.

Joyce Baldwin writes:

> Only when both parents remain faithful to their marriage vows can the children be given the security which provides the basis for godly living. The family was intended to be the school in which God's way of life was practiced and learned ... .[1]

John Benton says of the Lord:

> He is seeking godly offspring. He is looking for our children to become disciples. Of course, there is no guarantee that children of Christian parents will automatically embrace the faith of their parents... But we must realize that an unhappy Christian marriage, where the thought life (and therefore probably the words and actions) of the partners is far from perfect harmony, will be a profound obstacle to our children becoming Christians.[2]

Benton further writes:

> Our marriages are like a fig tree from which our Lord is expecting fruit. Our marriages are not just for us. They are for the Lord. Does he come to our marriages expecting to find refreshing fruit, but like that fig tree in the Gospels find none, though he had every reason to expect fruit? Why does he find no fruit? Sometimes it is *not* the Christian parents' fault that

children rebel. We are all sinners. But sometimes a heavy responsibility for the child's rebellion against the things of God lies with the parents. Sometimes it is the parents' fault. They have brought the name of God into disrepute with the child through what the child has seen in the marriage. This is terribly serious and we should not be surprised that God withdraws[3] (italics are his).

All of these things make treacherous dealing in marriage a very serious and weighty thing indeed. Thank God, we don't have to leave it there. Malachi also gives us

The remedy for treacherous dealing

Twice in this passage Malachi urges his people to 'take heed' to their spirits so that they would not 'deal treacherously' (vv. 15,16).

In these words, the prophet registers his conviction that the problem of unfaithfulness is rooted in man's spirit or heart. This is a much-needed corrective. We live in an age when people seek to excuse their unfaithfulness on the basis of their circumstances. But Malachi will have none of this. Unfaithfulness in every area of life flows from a heart that is not right with God. For this reason, the author of Proverbs urges:

Keep your heart with all
   diligence,
For out of it spring the issues
   of life
(Prov. 4:23).

If our hearts are not right with God, there's only one way to get them right and that is by repentance of sin. Repentance is necessary for the sinner to become a Christian, and repentance is necessary for the Christian who has strayed from the Lord.

The men of Malachi's generation had a clear and distinct law from God regarding marriage. Now the question before these men was what would they do about that law? Would they resent it and fly in the face of it? Or would they submit to it?

No words could be more vital for us. We know what God wants from our homes. We know he wants husbands and wives to be faithful to each other. We know that he wants us to practise Christian kindness and courtesy in our homes. We know that he wants us to rear our children to love and serve him.

But we live in a culture that ridicules and scorns these things, and, if we are not careful, we can become so enamoured and infatuated with our culture that we find ourselves resenting the commands of God and adopting the standards of our society. Take heed, child of God, that you do not develop a resentful spirit towards the teachings of God's Word!

FOR FURTHER STUDY

1. Marriage has been described as a 'creation ordinance'. Read Genesis 2:18-24. What does this passage teach about marriage?

2. Read Matthew 12:33-35. What do these verses tell us about the human heart?

TO THINK ABOUT AND DISCUSS

1. Why does God require believers to marry other believers?

2. How would you use passages in Scripture such as these to help a friend or family member who is a Christian yet is in a serious romantic relationship with an unbeliever?

3. What are some reasons why so many Christians are having trouble in their marriages? What are some ways in which we can guard our hearts?

For further study ▶

7 Cynicism towards God

(2:17 - 3:5)

To be cynical is to be scornful of the motives, virtue or integrity of someone. Some people are just cynical by nature; they're just plain cranky. I remember reading about a man who had a large, bushy moustache. While he was sleeping, some young pranksters smeared limburger cheese on his moustache. When he awoke his first comment was, 'This room stinks!' He immediately went into another room and pronounced: 'This house stinks.' He then stepped outside, and sniffed, and muttered, 'The whole world stinks!'

I've known some people who thought the whole world stank when the real trouble was right beneath their own noses! There is not much anyone can do with a person who insists on seeing the dark cloud behind every silver lining.

All cynicism is sad. But one type of cynicism is sadder than all the rest, and that is cynicism towards God, the only one who has never done anything to deserve it. And the saddest cynicism towards God is that which comes from people who profess to know and love him.

Malachi was not about to let such complacent cynicism go unchallenged. He sought to jerk his people back to reality by showing them both the reality of their cynicism and God's response to it.

Their cynicism (2:17)

The reasons for it

Why do people get cynical towards God? It is because they construct some notion of what he must do and when he must do it. If it does not happen according to their preconceived notion, they conclude that he has failed. Malachi's people were upset with God because, in their opinion, he had not corrected things that were crying for attention.

This complaint was their way of expressing unhappiness with God for not sending the Messiah. To their minds the Messiah was overdue. It was so clear to them, but it had not happened. Although God had demonstrated throughout their nation's history that he would be faithful to his promises, their faith in him was shaken. They took God's delay in fulfilling his promise to mean he was not going to keep his promise. So they thought he had let them down.

The result of it

Malachi leaves no doubt about the seriousness of their cynicism. He says it had 'wearied the LORD.'

Most of us are not accustomed to the idea of God getting tired. We think of the words of the prophet Isaiah: 'Have you not known? Have you not heard? The everlasting God, the LORD, the creator of the ends of the earth neither faints nor is weary' (Isa. 40:28).

Or we think of the psalmist's affirmation: ' ... He who

keeps you will not slumber. Behold, he who keeps Israel shall neither slumber nor sleep' (Ps. 121:3-4).

So we find ourselves wondering how Malachi could say that the Lord is wearied. There is really no contradiction. Isaiah and David were talking about the Lord not getting tired as he goes about his work. God ceaselessly watches over creation and works out his purposes without the slightest hint of exhaustion.

Malachi, on the other hand, was talking about the Lord getting tired or weary of putting up with unbelief among his people. God is great in patience, but he does, at length, get weary of seeing his people persist in sin.

Parents are familiar with this kind of tiredness. Some of their most frequently uttered words are, 'How many times do I have to tell you … !'

We obviously should not attribute to the Lord the same kind of impatience and anger that we are so prone to express, but we must recognize that the Lord's weariness with the sin of unbelief rises from the many demonstrations of his trustworthiness and his many warnings about unbelief.

Think about some of the times God proved his trustworthiness in the history of Israel. He had promised to deliver their forefathers from their bondage in Egypt (Exod. 6:5-8), and this he did. God had promised to drive the Canaanite nations out of the land of Palestine so Israel could inhabit it again (Deut. 7:22-26; 9:1-6), and this he did. God had promised to bring judgement upon his own people if they did not obey him (Deut. 28:15-68), and this he did again and again.

The generation to which Malachi spoke was not far

removed from a remarkable fulfilment of God's promise. After spending years in captivity, many of their own number had been restored to their land according to the promise of God.

In the light of these things, we wonder how these people could have had the audacity to suggest that God had failed to keep his promise regarding the Messiah. But they took God's delay in fulfilling his promise to mean he was not going to keep his promise. Many today make the same mistake about Christ's second coming. They look at the 'signs of the times', fix a date, and then get disillusioned with God when the date passes. Let us remember that we do not have God's wisdom and that God does not reckon time as we do (2 Peter 3:8-9). If we forget these things, our faith will be shaken and we shall make ourselves tiresome to God.

The Lord's response (3:1-5)

The certainty of the Messiah's coming (v. 1)

The Lord here assures his people that he has not forgotten his promise to send the Messiah. The one whom they were seeking would be preceded by a special messenger from God (John the Baptist). John Benton writes: 'John the Baptist was like a herald going before the royal procession to indicate the route that the king would take and to make preparations for his coming.'[1]

Furthermore, the Messiah would 'suddenly come to his temple.' The Lord probably chose to emphasize this because of the attitude that the people had towards the temple that had been rebuilt after the captivity. Because it could not compare with their first temple, built by Solomon, many were disappointed. Here the Lord tells them that their temple would have a glory all its own, a glory which could not be matched even by Solomon's. Their temple would be visited by the Messiah himself!

We should note that the Messiah is identified as 'the Messenger of the covenant'. He would come proclaiming a new covenant (Jer. 31:31; Ezek. 37:26).

We must not think that the Lord Jesus came to offer a new or different plan of salvation from that which had been previously known. This is, in fact, the view some hold. They see God trying one plan of salvation and then another, only finally to 'hit on' the idea of sending his Son.

The truth is that God has only had one plan of salvation in all of human history, and that plan is the Lord Jesus. The people of the Old Testament era were saved by looking forward in faith to his coming, and those since are saved by looking backward in faith to the Christ who has come. But all are saved by faith in Christ.

The newness of the covenant Jesus proclaimed is not due to it bringing in blessings that people had never experienced before. It is rather to be found in the degree to which these blessings were understood and enjoyed and the way in which those blessings were to be administered. With regard to the administration, the plan of salvation is the same under the old covenant and the new, that is, faith in the perfect sacrifice of Christ. But under the old, that salvation had to be continually anticipated through the sacrifice of animals. It is enjoyed under the new as a permanently purchased possession.

Verse 1, then, brings together three messengers. Malachi was proclaiming God's message of a messenger (John the Baptist), who would precede the greatest of all messengers (the Lord Jesus).

The character of the Messiah's coming (vv. 2-5)

The hearts of the people may very well have leaped within them as they heard Malachi assure them that the Messiah would come to their temple. They could not have been elated for long. The reason? Malachi proceeded to deliver a stinging message. Yes, the Messiah was coming, but he would not do what they were expecting. He would come to deal with the sins of Israel!

Malachi makes this point by saying that the Messiah would come 'like a refiner's fire' and 'like fullers' soap' (v. 2). As the refiner removes impurities from silver and the fuller (launderer) removes filth from clothes, so the Messiah would come to cleanse. And this cleansing work would apply to all. Even the religious leaders ('the sons of Levi'—v. 3) would not be exempt from it. The Messiah

> The truth is that God has only had one plan of salvation in all of human history, and that plan is the Lord Jesus. The people of the Old Testament era were saved by looking forward in faith to his coming, and those since are saved by looking backward in faith to the Christ who has come. But all are saved by faith in Christ.

would purify them so they would give 'an offering in righteousness' (v. 3).

Furthermore, the Messiah would come in the capacity of 'a swift witness' against sorcerers, adulterers, perjurers and oppressors of the helpless (v. 5). In other words, the Messiah would not delay in confronting such people with their sins.

To state it another way, the coming of the Lord would only bring trouble to those who were in the grip of cynical unbelief, for the Lord would come only to judge and purify them. Malachi's generation did not understand that the coming of the Lord would only be a comfort to those who were ready for it, that is, to those with hearts of faith. They thought when the Lord came, he would straighten out everyone except his own people. They did not realize that he would start obliterating evil by taking dead aim on the hearts of his own cold, unbelieving people!

Was Malachi on target in this prophecy? We only have to look at the Gospels to see that he was. When Jesus came, he made no move to overthrow the Roman government and to restore Israel to the position she had enjoyed under David and Solomon. Rather, he came calling his own people and the religious leaders to repent (Matt. 4:17; 23:1-39), and insisting that his kingdom was not of this world (Luke 17:21; John 18:36).

What does all this mean for us? It warns us about getting cynical towards God. Such cynism tires God and troubles us. Malachi's message also warns us about dictating to God. Many are doing with Christ's second coming what Malachi's people were doing with his first coming. People are setting dates and detailing all the specifics of Christ's return, but the real question is this: Are we ready for his return? To put it another way: Are our hearts filled with faith? That's what he will look for when he comes.

For further study ▶

FOR FURTHER STUDY

1. Read John 11:1-6. Why did Jesus delay in going to Bethany?
2. Read Matthew 10:34-39. How did Jesus describe his purpose in coming to this earth?

TO THINK ABOUT AND DISCUSS

1. Why does God sometimes delay in doing those things that his people expect?
2. The ministry of Jesus fulfilled the prophecy of Malachi. What is your response to Jesus' fulfilment of Old Testament prophecies?
3. How would you respond to a person in your neighbourhood or church who professed to have special insight—beyond that of most other believers—into the times relating to the return of Christ?

8 A dialogue about returning

(3:6-12)

Dialogue between God and Israel is the special feature of the prophecy of Malachi. The dialogue in these verses revolves around the word 'return'. It consists of five major elements.

The Lord calls for his people to return (vv.6-7a)

The Lord begins this plea by assuring the people that he has not changed (v. 6). Change can only go in one of two directions, that is, becoming better or worse. The Lord can do neither. He cannot become better because he is already perfect, and he cannot become worse because he can in no way deteriorate or become less than he already is.

The Lord also points out that the people of Israel had not changed (v. 7). They were disobeying him as their forefathers had done, but the unchanging nature of the Lord would not allow him to destroy them. He had committed himself to Israel, and he must keep his promise. His unchanging nature also guaranteed that he would return to them if they would return to him. Once again, it was a matter of God being faithful to his promises.

We are dealing with the same unchanging God who

requires obedience and who forgives those who repent of disobedience (1 John 1:9). In a world of flux and change, he is the constant.

The people refuse (v.7b)

When the people heard the Lord's message, they asked, 'In what way shall we return?'

We should not take this to mean that they were sincerely asking for guidance on the matter of returning to the Lord. Far from it! They were essentially saying, 'With reference to what sin should we return?' In other words, they were saying, 'We have not done anything!'

Miles Bennett offers this explanation:

> Their answer to God's gracious invitation to return proved how completely their self-righteousness had blinded them to their own spiritual condition. With hypocritical self-justification, they pretended an ignorance of any short-comings of conduct that called for repentance. [1]

The Lord answers their question (v. 8)

The people had asked what they had done to necessitate a return to God. With several things from which to choose, the Lord focused on one. They had been robbing him!

This shocking accusation only led to another insolent response: 'In what way have we robbed you?' (v. 8).

The Lord was ready with the answer: 'In tithes and offerings' (v. 8). A robbery can only take place if we take from someone something that belongs to him or her. God is plainly declaring that the tithe belongs to him. If the tithe belongs to him, and we use it for ourselves, what else can it be called except robbery?

John Benton suggests another way in which people can rob God:

> We can rob God by trying to keep time mostly to ourselves—time that should be given to God in personal prayer; time that should be given to God in family praise and worship; time that should be given to God in serving the needs of the local expression of the body of Christ.[2]

> **As is always the case, sin has consequences. The result of this sin was already in effect in that their fields were not giving them a good yield (v. 11).**

God announces a curse (v. 9)

The robbery of which God charged them had been done on a very wide scale. It was not just a few isolated instances. The Lord says the 'whole nation' was guilty.

As is always the case, sin has consequences. The result of this sin was already in effect in that their fields were not giving them a good yield (v. 11). This reminds us of what the prophet Haggai had said a few years earlier:

> You have sown much,
>   and bring in little;
> You eat, but do not have
>   enough;
> You drink, but you are not

> filled with drink;
> You clothe yourselves,
>> but no one is warm;
> And he who earns wages,
> Earns wages to put into a bag
>> with holes
> (Hag. 1:6).

God promises blessing (vv. 10-12)

The blessing of abundance (vv. 10-11)

Renewed obedience would lead to renewed blessing. The curse on the fields would be lifted. God would rebuke the devourer (v. 11), that is, the locusts which had been eating the crops.

The Lord urges the people to 'prove' him in this promise (v. 10). Let them return to God and check it out for themselves. God assures them that their blessing would be so great that it would be as if he had opened to them the very windows of heaven. It would be so abundant that there would not be 'room enough to receive it' (v. 10).

The blessing of influence (v. 12)

Israel's neighbours knew that she was a nation like no other and that the God with whom she was in covenant was a God like no other. They were, therefore, always mindful of what was going on in Israel and always drawing conclusions about Israel and her God. Sadly, Israel often gave the impression that the Lord was not real and that she was not unique. When she did so, God would bring judgement upon her to prove those very things. At this time, the nation was again giving her neighbours the wrong ideas. But if she were to return, those very neighbours would consider her to be both 'blessed' and 'a delightful land'.

Surely, we are driven to ask ourselves a very disturbing question. Can outsiders see God's hand of blessing on us? Does this not explain why our evangelistic efforts have such little impact? If God's hand of blessing were obvious in our lives, unbelievers would be beating a path to our door. But God does not bless disobedience, and disobedience is rampant among Christians. Failure to contribute financially is one act of disobedience that deprives us of God's good hand of blessing with all its evangelistic potential.

Christians sometimes debate whether the tithe of the Old Testament is still required, but we cannot debate whether we are to give generously. The apostle Paul makes this plain (2 Cor. 8:1-9:15). He also shows us that our giving must ever be tied to the love of God in Christ (2 Cor. 8:9; 9:15).

If we look at our bank accounts, we might very well find reasons not to give. But if we look (as we should) at the cross of Christ, we cannot help but give.

For further study ▶

1. Read Hosea 14:1-4. What does this passage teach us about returning to God?

2. Read Matthew 6:1-4 and 2 Corinthians 8:1-9:15. What do these passages teach us about the matter of giving?

TO THINK ABOUT AND DISCUSS

1. What does God's plea for his people to return to him tell you about him? What does this mean to you?

2. Think about some ways in which God's work could be advanced by his people giving more generously. Think about your own spending. What can you do to 'free up' more of your money for the Lord's work?

3. How would this passage help you to deal with a relatively wealthy fellow Christian believer who struggles to maintain a disciplined attitude to finance and who expresses the view that he or she does not consider systematic and regular giving to the church to be a requirement under New Testament teaching?

9 The listening God

(3:13-18)

These verses focus our attention on God's awareness of everything people say. Such knowledge, along with the realization that words will be judged by God (Matt. 12:36-37), should make us very careful!

God listening to words of complaint (vv. 13-15)

The Lord confronts them (v. 13)

The Lord charges the people of Israel with speaking harshly against him (v. 13), and, as they did with each of his previous charges, the people dispute the charge by asking, 'What have we spoken against you?' That amounted to them saying, 'We have done no such thing!' They did not seem to realize that their quarrelling with God proved his point!

The Lord quotes them (vv. 14-15)

God proceeds to show them how they had spoken against him. No, they had not said: 'God is bad' or 'God is mean.' But they had said: 'It is vain to serve God' (v. 14).

As the Lord continues to quote their own words to them,

we cannot help but conclude that they were taking too much credit. They claim that they had 'kept his ordinance', that is, obeyed his commands. They also profess to have 'walked as mourners' before the Lord. As John Benton points out, mourners at a funeral are 'careful to be on their best behaviour.'[1]

The people were claiming to have been very well behaved and very careful about serving the Lord!

After all this faithful, careful serving they had supposedly done, they draw the monstrous conclusion that it is better to be wicked than to be righteous! (v. 15). The proud are more blessed than the humble! The wicked are built up while the righteous are torn down! Those who thumb their noses at God get away with it!

Others in the Bible came to this same melancholy conclusion. Asaph, the author of Psalm 73, writes:

> But as for me,
>   my feet had almost stumbled;
> My steps had nearly slipped.
> For I was envious of the
>   boastful,
> When I saw the prosperity of
>   the wicked
> (Ps. 73:2-3).

A bit later he adds:

> Behold, these are the ungodly,
> Who are always at ease;

They increase in riches.
Surely I have cleansed my
    heart in vain,
And washed my hands in
    innocence.
For all day long I have been
    plagued,
And chastened every morning
(Ps. 73:12-14).

Many believers today have no trouble identifying with Asaph! We cannot come away from this section without asking ourselves if we are as guilty as Malachi's people. Do we claim too much for ourselves in terms of serving the Lord? Do we suggest by the way that we go about the Lord's work that it is a very dreary and meaningless affair? Do we find ourselves envying those who are not 'burdened' with serving the Lord? Do we yearn to be free from serving the Lord? If we speak against serving God, we have spoken against God!

God listening to words of encouragement (vv. 16-18)

Who spoke these words?

Malachi describes them as 'those who fear the LORD' and 'meditate on his name' (v. 16). What does it mean to fear God? It is to stand in awe of his person, to submit to his authority and to dread his displeasure. Christians are not casual or nonchalant about God!

We should note that Malachi simply states this as a fact.

He does not say the righteous should fear the Lord, but, in a matter-of-fact way, he observes that they do.

If this is true of the righteous, it is simple logic that the unrighteous do not fear the Lord. The Bible flatly asserts this: 'There is no fear of God before their eyes' (Rom. 3:18).

The ungodly refuse to be afraid of God when there is reason to be afraid.

To whom did they speak and what did they say?

These people spoke to 'one another'. Those who feared the Lord spoke to others who feared the Lord. John Benton writes:

> Some people realized that if they went on much longer in this climate of conversation, where all they heard poured scorn on God, then very soon they too would end up bitter and faithless. Their response was to seek each other out and to talk together.[2]

While the text does not specify what these people said, the fact that they all feared the Lord means they spoke words consistent with that fear and words that would encourage and promote it.

What resulted from their speaking?

THE LORD PROMISES TO REMEMBER THEM (V. 16)

The Jews were familiar with the idea of kings recording the names of those who had done good (Esth. 6:1-2). God also has such a book. It consists of the names of the God-fearers of whom he has been speaking. We are not to conclude from this that God has a bad memory. It is rather God stooping to their level to speak in a way they could easily understand. He was assuring them that he will not forget those who do not forget him! The God with perfect memory keeps perfect records!

THE LORD PROMISES A SPECIAL PRIVILEGE (V. 17)

The Lord will not only remember these people but also treat them as his own special treasure on that glorious day when he makes up his jewels. The thought is that God's people are jewels who are scattered and mired in the mud of this world. But at the end, he will find them all, put them into his treasure chest and will look upon them with pride and satisfaction. They will be his crown jewels. God's people may not appear to be much now, but they will be known to be much then (see Dan. 12:3).

THE LORD PROMISES A CLEAR DISTINCTION (V. 18)

The difference between believers and unbelievers may not always be apparent in this life, but, in the words of T. V. Moore, there is coming a ' … great day of final adjustment … in which all seeming anomalies of the present shall be fully explained and wholly removed forever.'[3]

What day is this great day? It is the day when this life is over and eternity finally dawns.

On that day, the debate about whether it is wise to serve God will cease for ever. To the people of Malachi's day, it often appeared that there was no point in being righteous. The line between the righteous and the wicked was so horribly blurred that it seemed as if one was as good as another. But eternity will bring clarity to all muddled situations, and it will be obvious that the righteous were wise. Like the people of Malachi's generation, we sometimes envy the wicked, but no one will envy them in eternity.

We may not be able to detect much difference between the righteous and the wicked here. They may appear to be equally blessed and in some instances the wicked may appear to be even more blessed. But when the eternal day dawns, the difference will be plain for all to see.

The people of God are not to expect him to vindicate them finally in this life. We get into deep trouble when we expect this life to yield the things that only eternity can yield.

We are further called not to envy the wicked but to feel deep compassion and pity for them. The happiness they enjoy in this life is all the happiness they will know. Asaph was at first troubled by the prosperity of the wicked, but he came to see that it is utter foolishness to envy anyone who is headed for eternal destruction (Ps. 73:17-20).

FOR FURTHER STUDY

1. Read Psalm 94:1-7. How does the psalmist describe the wicked?
2. Read Deuteronomy 32:10. What is the name given here for the people of God?

TO THINK ABOUT AND DISCUSS

1. God hears all our words. What does this mean to you? How might this affect the way in which you speak both in private and in public in the fellowship of your church? In the light of the teaching of James in the New Testament (See James 3:1-12), what steps might you consider taking in order to develop a better use of your tongue?

2. What comforts you when you are inclined to think that the wicked are faring better than the righteous? How could you use the principle from Malachi's teaching to help someone who is not yet a Christian to understand how God still works out all things for the good of those who love him and have been called according to his purpose (Rom. 8:28 f)?

10 The coming day

(4:1-6)

These verses contain four references to a future day (vv. 1,3,5). There can be no doubt that Malachi was referring to the day which he mentioned in the last verse of chapter 3, that is, the Day of Judgement.

What will that day be like? (vv. 1-3)

We do not like to hear about the theme of judgement, and we may rest assured that Malachi's people found it distasteful as well. But the fact that we do not like the matter does not make it go away. One who is stricken with serious illness does not suddenly become well because he finds illness to be unpleasant! We can deny and ignore judgement as much as we want, but Malachi's words are still true: 'the day is coming' (v. 1).

It will be a day of calamity for the wicked (v. 1)

Judgement Day will mean different things for different people. For the wicked it will be horrible beyond description. That day is like a burning oven, and the wicked are like stubble. When the stubble hits the oven, it is burned, and when the wicked hit judgement, they are consumed.

This imagery is not Malachi's alone. It is found in many Scriptures and, most notably, in the teaching of the Lord Jesus Christ (Matt. 3:12; 13:30; Mark 9:43-49; Luke 16:19-31; John 15:6).

The outcome of Judgement Day for the wicked is complete destruction. They will be left with 'neither root nor branch'. Charles D. Isbell writes: 'Nothing will be left of them. No hope will exist for them. No future. No brighter day. All will be over, consumed in the mighty fire of God.'[1]

The opening verses of Luke 12 relate an episode in which 'an innumerable multitude' gathered together to hear Jesus.

Having perfect knowledge of all people (John 2:23-25), Jesus knew this multitude. He knew these people were living as if this life is all there is and as if losing it is the ultimate calamity. He knew that they were living as if there were no eternity.

So Jesus spoke to them about the ultimate calamity. It was not physical death (Luke 12:4).

It was rather being 'cast into hell' (Luke 12:5)!

The word translated 'hell' is the Greek word 'Gehenna'. The word was the city refuse dump where the fires unceasingly burned. It is a frightening representation of that which awaits those without God.

The one who 'has power to cast into hell' is not Satan, as some have suggested. It is God.

Some get confused on the matter of the killing of the body. In verse 4, Jesus mentions 'those who kill the body.' In verse 5, he says, 'Fear him who, after he has killed, has power to cast into hell.' So, who does the killing of the body? Is it God or others? The answer is 'both'. In other words, no matter how we die, it is in keeping with God's appointment and with his knowledge and permission.

But the key thing, as Jesus so powerfully proclaims, is not the killing of the body but that which comes next!

There is much about hell that we do not know. But here are some things we do know:

- It is a real place
- It is a place of separation from God and all that is good (Luke 16:23)
  - It is a place of just punishment (Luke 16:24)
  - It is a place where there is memory (Luke 16:25)
  - It is a place of hopelessness (Luke 16:26)

Something else we know is that we do not have to go there. Those who confess the truth about Jesus will be saved (v.8). The coming day of judgement will be quite different for these! (Luke 12:8)

It will be a day of joy and triumph for the righteous (vv. 2-3)

That same day will bring unspeakable joy to the people of God. On that day, 'the Sun of Righteousness shall arise with healing in his wings' (v. 2). The Lord Jesus, who often seems in eclipse, will shine forth in all his brilliance. And his 'wings' ('rays') will touch all his people, bringing warmth and healing them of all their diseases.

On that day, the people of God will be like calves, who having been released into the sunshine from their dingy stalls, kick up their heels in sheer exuberance.

And on that day, the righteous will be vindicated. Those who are so often trampled by the wicked here will triumph over them then.

What must we do to prepare for that day? (vv. 4-6)

Remember the Law (v. 4)

Malachi once again calls the people to adhere faithfully to the Law of Moses. It was, in fact, the law that God gave to and through Moses. This is a reference to the Ten Commandments in which God lays out their duties to him and one another. We must not think, however, that we can be saved from our sins and prepared for Judgement Day by keeping these commandments. God gave them, not as a way of salvation, but rather to serve as a mirror that shows us our sinfulness. It is very significant that having mentioned the law, Malachi immediately proceeds to the ministry of Christ.

> We must not think, however, that we can be saved from our sins and prepared for Judgement Day by keeping these commandments. God gave them, not as a way of salvation, but rather to serve as a mirror that shows us our sinfulness.

Flee to Christ (vv. 5-6)

Many find these verses to be confusing. Malachi has obviously been speaking of the Day of Judgement at the end of human history, but here he begins speaking about Elijah coming. We know that this is a prophecy of the ministry of John the Baptist (Matt. 11:11-14; 17:10-13), and we know that John the Baptist came to pave the way for Jesus (John 1:19-34).

So the question we are facing is this: How did Malachi get from Judgement Day to Jesus' day? John Benton gives this answer: ' … there is a sense in which the last day, the Day of Judgement, was brought forward and broke into history in the coming of Jesus.'[2]

He further writes:

> When people receive or reject the Lord Jesus Christ, they are passing judgement day verdict upon themselves. In preparing people for Jesus to be revealed to the nation of the Jews, John was preparing people for judgement day. Those who truly owned up to their sins would be looking for the Saviour. Those who went on in the pretence and hypocrisy of being good enough for God by their 'religion' would reject Jesus. That judgement stands for eternity.[3]

The upshot of it all is if we want to be prepared for Judgement Day, we must receive the Christ whose ministry pictured it and signalled it.

By the way, the ministry of John the Baptist would prove to have a profound effect on the family life of the people of Israel. It would turn the hearts of fathers towards their children and the hearts of the children towards their fathers. How we need such a turning! And that turning can come only as parents and children find a common bond in the Christ of whom John spoke. One of the evidences that people have truly found Christ is the love they have for one another. Where that love exists, there is blessing. Where it does not exist, there is a curse (v. 6).

For further study ▶

FOR FURTHER STUDY

1. Read Matthew 25:31-46. What does this passage teach about the final judgement?
2. Read Revelation 20:11-15. What does this passage teach about the final judgement?

TO THINK ABOUT AND DISCUSS

1. What is your response to the reality of God's judgement?
2. What is your response to God's provision of safety from judgement through Christ? How might this affect the way in which you live for him
In your employment or school situation
At church
In sharing the gospel with other people
3. How would such passages as the ones mentioned in this chapter help you to persuade a person that there is a judgement to come? Consider this in the light of Romans 1:16-32

Additional Resources

John Calvin, *Commentaries on the Twelve Minor Prophets,* vol. xv, Baker Book House

E. Ray Clendenen, *The New American Commentary,* vol. xxi (a), Broadman & Holman Publishers

John Gill, *Exposition of the Old & New Testaments,* vol. vi, The Baptist Standard Bearer

Stephen R. Miller, *Holman Old Testament Commentary,* vol. xx, Broadman & Holman Publishers

Endnotes

Background and summary

1 T. Miles Bennett, *The Broadman Bible Commentary; Malachi*, Broadman Press, vol. vii, p.368
2 Joyce G. Baldwin, *Tyndale Old Testament Commentaries: Haggai, Zechariah, Malachi*, p.211.
3 As above.
4 As above, p.216.

Chapter 1 —
Doubting God's love

1 Baldwin, *Malachi*, pp.222-3.

Chapter 2 —
Dishonouring God's name

1 John Benton, *Losing Touch with the Living God*, Evangelical Press, pp.27-8.
2 As above, p.30.

Chapter 3 —
More about dishonouring God's name

1 Benton, *Losing Touch*, p.53.

Chapter 4 —
Sinning against the name of the Lord

1 Bennett, *The Broadman Commentary*, p.380.

Chapter 5 —
Corrupting the covenant

1 Benton, *Losing Touch*, p.46.
2 As above, p.48.
3 Steven J. Lawson, *Famine in the Land*, Moody Publishers, p.82.
4 As above, pp.82-3.
5 Baldwin, *Malachi*, p.237.

Chapter 6 —
Dealing treacherously

1 Baldwin, *Malachi*, pp.240-1.
2 Benton, *Losing Touch*, p.79.
3 As above, p.80.

Chapter 7 —
Cynicism towards God

1 Benton, *Losing Touch*, p.92.

Chapter 8 —
A dialogue about returning

1 Bennett, *The Broadman Commentary*,
    p.390.
2 Benton, *Losing Touch*, p.105.

Chapter 9 —
The listening God

1 Benton, *Losing Touch*, p.112.
2 As above, p.117.
3 T.V. Moore, *Zechariah, Haggai &
    Malachi*, The Banner of Truth Trust,
    pp.167-8.

Chapter 10 —
The coming day

1 Charles D. Isbell, *Bible Study
    Commentary: Malachi*, Lamplighter
    Books, p.75.
2 Benton, *Losing Touch*, p.130.
3 As above.